THE ANN

named the Annunc
Solemnity, though
exclude the other.

In his Apostoli
(Devotion to Mary),
nine months before the Nativity, "East and West celebrate this solemnity as the commemoration of the fiat of the Incarnate Word who, entering the world, said, 'God, here I am! I am coming to do your will.' They commemorate the beginning of Redemption and the indissoluble and wedded union of the divine and human natures in the one Person of the Word. It is also a feast of the New Eve, the obedient, faithful virgin who, with her own fiat, became the Mother of God through the power of the Holy Spirit. It is the culmination of the dialogue of salvation between God and Man, and the commemoration of Mary's free consent and co-operation in the plan of redemption."

St Thomas Aquinas says that it was the Father's will that the Redemption of mankind should depend on the Son's adoption of human nature through the power of the Holy Spirit, and the consent of His mother Mary. This does not mean that the Trinity was dependent on the will of a creature, and that, otherwise, redemption would not have taken place, but that, from all eternity, Mary's consent was foreseen and therefore accepted in the divine plan of salvation. (cf. *'Lumen Gentium'* Dogmatic Constitution on the Church, Ch 8).

From the Liturgy

"Listen now, House of David: are you not satisfied with trying the patience of men without trying the patience of my God too? The Lord Himself, therefore, will give you a sign. It is this: the maiden is with child and will soon give birth to a son whom she will call Emmanuel which means God is with us." (*First Reading, Isaiah 7:10-14*).

"Bulls' blood and goats' blood are useless for taking away sins, and this is what Christ said upon coming into the world: 'You who wanted no sacrifice or oblation, prepared a body for me. You took no pleasure in holocausts or sacrifices for sin; then I said, just as I was commanded in the scroll of the book, 'God, here I am! I come to obey your will.'" (*Second Reading, Heb 10:5-7; cf. Ex 24:8*).

God sent the Angel Gabriel to Nazareth, a town in Galilee, to Mary, a virgin betrothed to Joseph who was of the House of David. He said "Hail, full of grace; the Lord is with you." Mary did not understand this greeting but the angel told her not to be afraid because she had found favour with God. She was going to conceive and bear a son through the power of the Holy Spirit. He would be called the Son of God and she must name Him Jesus. To show that nothing was beyond God's power, Gabriel told Mary that her elderly cousin Elizabeth, who had been infertile all her life, was now expecting her first baby. Mary declared that she was the Lord's handmaid and was willing to let everything happen just as the angel had said. Without a thought for herself, she

COMPANION TO THE FEASTS OF OUR LORD

by
J. B. Midgley

*All booklets are published thanks to the
generous support of the members of the
Catholic Truth Society*

CATHOLIC TRUTH SOCIETY
PUBLISHERS TO THE HOLY SEE

Contents

Introduction 3
The Annunciation of the Lord 4
The Nativity of the Lord 9
The Holy Family of Jesus, Mary and Joseph 15
The Circumcision of the Lord 23
The Most Holy Name of Jesus 27
The Epiphany of the Lord 32
The Presentation of the Lord 38
The Baptism of the Lord 43
The Transfiguration of the Lord 48
The Body and Blood of Christ 53
The Resurrection 58
The Ascension 64
The Sacred Heart of Jesus 69
Divine Mercy 74
The Triumph of the Cross 79
Christ the King 83
Acknowledgments 87
Chronological List of Feasts 88

Introduction

The original meaning of 'Liturgy', as a service in the name of the people, includes the People of God's participation in Our Lord's work of Redemption. In celebrating Divine Worship and proclaiming the Gospel, Church and faithful unite in His prayer to the Father and the exercise of His priestly office. The Liturgy, then, symbolises belief in the economy of salvation in which God's merciful designs are a prelude to their perfection in Christ.

The Second Vatican Council teaches that "the Liturgy is the summit towards which the activity of the Church is directed, and the fountain from which all its power flows." Among the Council's reforms was the restoration of the Feasts of Our Lord, with Sundays, to their central importance. (*'Sacrosanctum Concilium'*, Constitution on the Sacred Liturgy, 1963, n 5; 102-11). They adorn the Liturgy, trace Our Lord's steps on His mission in the New Covenant and signpost our journey which is life in Him. These pages are offered with the hope that they may provide a convenient accompaniment.

J.B. Midgley,
Downham Market, Pentecost 2002.

The Annunciation of the Lord

March 25th

Origins and significance

In ancient times there was a theory that March 25th was the date of Lucifer's downfall, the creation of Adam, Israel's escape through the parted waters of the Red Sea, and Our Lord's death upon the cross. Significantly, the old liturgical calendars identified it variously as the Feast of the Incarnation, the Beginning of the Redemption, the Annunciation of Christ, His conception by the Holy Spirit, and Lady Day in honour of His virgin Mother.

In the Eastern Church, this day was always a Feast of the Lord, and Mary's obedient co-operation in God's eternal plan of salvation was commemorated on December 26th, the day after she had given birth to God made Man. In the West, there were early mentions of the Feast in the Sacramentarium of St Gelasius, the first pope to be called Vicar of Christ, and in the records of the Synod of Toledo (696) which refer to the celebration of the Angel Gabriel's announcement of the Incarnation to the Blessed Virgin Mary. It became associated with the Mother rather than the Son, until, in the reordering of the Roman Calendar in 1969, it was set off immediately to help Elizabeth during the last three months of her pregnancy. (*cf. The Gospel, Lk 1:26-45*).

"He took the form of a servant without stain of sin. He enhanced our humanity without diminishing His divinity. The emptying by which the Invisible One made Himself visible, and by which the Lord and Creator of all things willed to be one with mortal men, was a bending down in pity, not a failure in power" (*Office of Readings, St Leo the Great, d.461*).

Reflection

The Emmanuel prophecy of the first reading informs the House of David that its deliverance is at hand in the person of the Word Incarnate, conceived and born of a virgin mother. She calls Him Emmanuel, God is with us, a name which in Hebrew usage implied the possession of Messianic characteristics and God's power to liberate His people. It was not customary for a mother to name a child but, in this case, the virginal conception makes the decision appropriate. The House of David represents humanity which is to be delivered from the shackles of sin and reconciled to God. In the second reading, Our Lord announces the replacement of ritual sacrifice by His own sacrificial obedience. He uses the words of a messianic psalm which is evocative of Samuel's obedient response, David's realisation that a pure heart and a humble spirit delight God more than burnt offerings, and Mary's fiat. Without love, the former sacrifices were of no value, and it is the Son's perfect offering which is pleasing and efficacious. (*cf. 1 Sam 3:10; Ps 40:6, 51:16-19*).

Nazareth was a hillside village twenty miles west of Tiberias, and so insignificant that it did not warrant a mention either in Josephus' History or the Talmud, the corpus of Jewish ceremonial and civil law. The inhabitants were spoken of with some contempt, as when Nathanael, the future Apostle Bartholomew, when told about Jesus by Philip, asked if anything good could come from such a place. In this unpromising location the plan of salvation was initiated when God sent Gabriel with the news of the Incarnation, the most momentous event in history. The prophecies that Jesus would be called a Nazarene, and grow up in an environment far from glorious in the eyes of the world, were fulfilled. It would, however, be immortalised in Pilate's notice of execution, "Jesus of Nazareth, King of the Jews." (*cf. Mt 2:23; Isaiah 53; Ps 21; Jn 1:46; 19:19*).

We might be fearful or bewildered about God's plan for us, or fail to recognise comfort in submission. Then we remember that Jesus and Mary include us in their willingness to accept the Father's intentions, so that His designs come to fruition as we are embraced in their obedience to the divine will which begins salvation. The love and compassion God showed "His servant in her lowliness" is extended to us with whom Mary shares her magnanimity in welcoming the Saviour.

The Nativity of the Lord

December 25th

Origins and significance

Pope Liberius preached a sermon on 'The Birthday of Christ' in St Peter's in 353AD, the earliest indication of the Feast's institution. By the end of the fourth century it figured in liturgical calendars throughout the West where, until the tenth century, it marked the beginning of the ecclesiastical year. The general acceptance of December 25th as the date of our Lord's Birthday also determined the dates of the Annunciation, the Birthday of John the Baptist, the Circumcision, and the Presentation. Initially, the Coming of the Magi was celebrated with the Nativity until January 6th became the Feast of the Epiphany. The Second Council of Tours, 567AD, recommended that Advent should be a period of fasting as a worthy preparation for December 25th, and drew attention to the sanctity of the twelve days between the Nativity and the Epiphany. Apparently, celebrations were becoming too enthusiastic and 'The Laws of King Cnut' of Denmark, 1100AD, for example, had to order a fast during this period to restrain "popular merry-making".

Three Masses composed for the Liturgy of the Nativity to be celebrated at midnight, dawn, and in the day, were seen by St Thomas Aquinas as the mystical representation of Our Lord's three births in eternity, time, and in the human soul. It was early papal practice to celebrate the first in the church of St Mary Major, the second in St Anastasia's as a mark of honour to the Eastern Church, and the third in St Peter's. One of the earliest Nativity hymns used in celebrations is *'Corde Natus ex Parentis'*, by the Spanish poet Aurelius (d.413AD), who is the only lay Father of the Church.

"O that ever blessed birthday
> when the Virgin full of grace,
Of the Holy Ghost, incarnate
> bare the Saviour of our race.
And that child, the world's Redeemer,
> first displayed His sacred face."

Preparations for the Incarnation

When Mary returned to Nazareth after the birth of John the Baptist (*cf. The Annunciation of the Lord and Lk 1:26-45*), her own condition was plain for all to see. Joseph found himself in a painful situation because any apparent act of infidelity during the betrothal period was considered as adultery. As a pious Jew, he was well acquainted with the law which sought to protect the honour of the House of Israel by condemning an adulterous woman to death by stoning, and he knew that, as the wronged husband, he would be called upon to cast the first stone. (*cf. Deut*

22:23). He thought about completing the marriage and acknowledging the child as his own, but such a deception gave him qualms of conscience, and he decided on another course. Though he was the injured party, he was not obliged to denounce Mary before the village tribunal, so it seemed best to issue a private bill of divorce in front of two witnesses without going to court. That night, as Joseph slept, Gabriel told him to have no misgivings about taking Mary home as his wife because the child she was carrying had been conceived through the power of the Holy Spirit. He was to have legal guardianship and undertake the paternal responsibility of naming the Child 'Jesus' because he would save the people from their sins.

The Birth of Our Lord

Six months later, Caesar Augustus called for a census of the population to calculate the revenue available from taxation. Every citizen had to register in the place of family origin and for Joseph, who was of the royal House of David, this involved a sixty mile journey from Nazareth to Bethlehem five miles south of Jerusalem. A wife was not obliged to register with her husband, but Mary went with Joseph and one can understand why this devoted couple wanted to be together. Also, their obedience to earthly authority helped realise God's promise that the Saviour would be born in Bethlehem. (*cf. Mi 5:1*). Mary knew that the time of her confinement was imminent because she took with her swaddling clothes in which to wrap a newborn infant. No sooner had they arrived in the city where David had been born and anointed king of Israel, than she went into labour. The number of people coming for registration had put a strain on accommodation, and the only lodging Joseph could find was an animal shelter. In such uncongenial surroundings the Son of God came into the world, was wrapped in the swaddling clothes of a helpless baby, and cradled in a feeding box.

The Shepherds

Judaea was sheep-rearing country and Bethlehem itself a centre for the shepherds who tended their masters' flocks. On the night of Jesus' birth, some were guarding their sheep when the Angel appeared, radiant in the Lord's own glorious light. He calmed their fears, told them the wonderful news of the Saviour's birth and gave them directions as to where they could find Him. A heavenly choir of angels joined God's messenger in praising Him and announced peace to all people of good will.

The penalties exacted for abandonment or loss of sheep were severe, so it was with admirable faith that the shepherds hurried down to Bethlehem where they found Mary, Joseph, and the Baby lying in a manger, just as the angel had said. They repeated everything he had told them and, with this confirmation of the Annunciation's details, Mary and Joseph began to treasure in their hearts the assurance that the Baby was the Redeemer who had entered the world of men. The shepherds returned to their duties and, as they went praised and thanked God because they had found the Truth about whom the angel had spoken.

Extreme poverty and the nature of their work caused shepherds to live on the fringes of society, even on the edge of the law. Conventional people regarded them with suspicion and the Rabbinical class was critical of a lifestyle which was incompatible with exact observance of religious regulations. However, it was not to kings, potentates, or professional religious leaders that the angels first announced Creation's most important news. While the world slept, God showed His love for the humble as He invited attentive shepherds to be first visitors to His Son who would call Himself the Good Shepherd. From the beginning, it is to the poor that the Good News of the Kingdom is proclaimed. (*cf.Mt 1:18-25; Lk 2:1-20*).

From the Liturgy

"In the beginning was the Word: the Word was with God and the Word was God. He was with God in the beginning...all that came to be had life in Him and that life was the light of men...that shines in the dark...that darkness could not overcome. The Word was made flesh and came to dwell among us, and we saw His glory...as the only Son of the Father, full of grace and truth." (*Gospel, Mass during the Day, Jn 1:1-15*).

"He is the radiant light of God's glory and the perfect copy of His nature, sustaining the universe by His powerful command." (*Second Reading, Heb 1:1-6*).

Reflection

The omnipotent work of creating existence from nothing is the Father's; the omnipotent work of wisdom in ordering the universe is that of the Son. Adam's sin had disturbed the order so it was right that the Son, the new Adam, should restore order by becoming man and mediating a new covenant. It was not the Trinity but the Word proceeding from the Father who became man to effect the world's redemption. When He came to earth in the Person of Our Lord Jesus Christ, He did not separate Himself from the Godhead. The unity of the divine essence in the relationship of the Trinity remained unaltered. God the Son, already existed in His divine nature when He took human nature in Mary's womb, not through paternal action but by the power of the Holy Spirit. He developed in the womb like any other baby and, in due time, was born into the world, entering history to share the frailty of human nature in every way except sin. In joining the human family, He made us children of God and sharers in His divinity. "He came to dwell" is better translated by the biblical idiom "He fixed His tent", in that He did not make earth His permanent dwelling place, but He does not leave us orphans.

THE HOLY FAMILY OF JESUS, MARY AND JOSEPH

*Sunday in the Octave of Christmas,
or December 30th if no Sunday intervenes.*

Origins and significance

In the Liturgy, Our Lord and His Blessed Mother receive the most profound veneration. Devotion to His Fosterfather is also inspired by the Holy Spirit who prompted St Matthew to describe Joseph as a "just man", an epithet which epitomises every virtue. By the end of the third century, his feast was being celebrated in the Coptic Church, and a magnificent altar had been dedicated to him in the basilica built by St Helena, the mother of the emperor Constantine. Formal liturgical celebration of a Feast of the Holy Family came later when it was first inaugurated in Canada in the seventeenth century. There was strong encouragement from Pope Leo XIII (d.1903) and Pope Benedict XV who, in 1921 shortly before he died, decreed that the Mass composed for the Feast should be celebrated throughout the universal Church.

The Entrance Antiphon of the Feast is "The shepherds hastened to Bethlehem where they found Mary and Joseph, and the Baby lying in a manger." *(Lk 2:16)*. This is the first picture of the Holy Family, and the beginning of their family life which was to continue in Nazareth. Pope Paul VI observed that "the Church meditates with profound reverence upon the holy life led in the house in Nazareth by Jesus, the Son of God, His Mother, and Joseph, the just man...There is a lesson in family life." The Pope prayed that Nazareth would teach us what family life is, its communion of love, its austere and simple beauty, and its sacred and inviolable character." He hoped that we would learn from the Holy Family that "the formation received at home is gentle and irreplaceable" in its contribution to social order. (*'Marialis Cultus', 1964*).

From the Liturgy

The opening prayer of the Feast praises God who crowned the goodness of creation with the family of man, and sent His Son to dwell in time, and conform to the laws of life in the world. The Church prays that, in the sanctity of human love and with appreciation of family life, we come to live in peace and share God's eternal life.

The Book of Ecclesiasticus, from which the first reading is taken, predates the Holy Family by two centuries but remains relevant to family life in every age, as parents share God's creative act in the transmission of life and the nurturing of personality. Their tenderness towards their offspring, especially when they can do nothing for themselves, reflects God's love for all His children, and this is the source from which their own love springs. Children have their own opportunity to be creative as they recognise the wonders which God works, and when age diminishes their parents' powers. "The Lord honours the father in his children and upholds the rights of a mother over her sons. Whoever respects his father is like someone amassing a fortune...He will be happy with children of his own and be heard on the day when he prays. Long life comes to him who honours his father; he who sets his mother at ease shows obedience to the Lord." (*Si 3:2-6; 12-14*).

In the second reading, St Paul outlines the pattern of relationships which God provides as the foundation of human society. The family, of which Jesus, Mary and Joseph, are the supreme example, mirrors our relationship with God in which loving obedience brings fulfilment, and it demonstrates His own love for the world revealed in Our Lord. "You are God's chosen race, His saints; He loves you and you should be clothed in sincere compassion, kindness, and humility, gentleness and patience. Bear with one another, forgive each other as soon as a quarrel begins. The Lord has forgiven you, now you must do the same. Teach and advise one another in all wisdom...and never say or do anything except in the name of the Lord Jesus, giving thanks to God the Father through Him." (*Col 3:12-21*).

We learn in the Gospel of the Feast (*Mt 2:13-15; 19-23*) that as Joseph slept, "the angel", and one likes to think it was still Gabriel in his co-ordinating role, told him to take his family to Egypt because Herod was intent on eliminating the Baby whom he regarded as a rival for his throne. It would have taken the Holy Family a fearful journey of five or six days to reach the frontiers of Egypt. This was now a prefecture of the Roman Empire and, with a Jewish population of about one million, had become a traditional sanctuary from any oppression encountered in Israel. Herod died at Passover in 4BC, so the exile lasted less than a year. The angel broke the news to Joseph in a dream and said he could now take Jesus and Mary back to Israel. The words of the prophet "When Israel was a child I loved him, and I called my son out of Egypt" (*Ho 11:1*), are resonant of Israel's exile, and the providential rehearsal for the Saviour's return to gather the scattered sheep of Israel, and show how faithful God is to His promises.

Joseph set off on the return journey intending to take the family to Bethlehem, either to live there or put his affairs in order. On the Egyptian-Gaza-Azotus road, he heard that Archelaus had succeeded Herod in Judaea which, because of his unsavoury reputation, was now a dangerous place for the Mesiah. A further dream-warning confirmed Joseph's fears, and he turned his steps towards Galilee where the less menacing Antipas ruled. The Holy Family made their home in Nazareth, though even here life would have its anxieties because the character of Herod Antipas did not inspire confidence. He it was who would subsequently be responsible for the murder of Jesus' cousin, John the Baptist, and would be in Jerusalem at the time of Our Lord's betrayal and arrest. He would treat Him with shameful ridicule before sending Him to Pilate for a travesty of judgement. Eleven years passed by.

Reflection

In March or April every year, the Jews celebrated the Feast of Passover which recalled Israel's delivery from Egyptian bondage. It was also the Feast of Unleavened Bread in memory of the meal which God had ordered to be prepared and eaten with all speed before the Exodus. People came from far and wide to celebrate the Feast in Jerusalem, and Jewish boys assumed this obligation as circumcised "sons of the Law" when they reached the age of twelve. Accordingly, Mary and Joseph took Jesus for His first conscious visit to the city and His Father's House since He had been a babe in arms, and it was an occasion of striking significance. On their way home, His parents were unaware that He had stayed in Jerusalem. Pilgrimages were composed of village groups with men and women travelling separately along the way, so either parent could innocently assume a child was safe within the other's group. Also, in eastern Mediterranean societies, twelve year old boys were well able to look after themselves and exercised a degree of independence. Only when Mary and Joseph stopped for the night after a day's walk, did the awful truth dawn on them that Jesus was missing. Sick with worry, they rushed back to Jerusalem where they searched frantically for three days before finding Him in the Temple conferring with legal experts who were astonished at His wisdom. Their relief was overwhelming, but naturally Mary asked Jesus why He had caused them so much heartache. His own question by way of reply bemused them. Why had they looked for Him when they should have known that He had to attend to His father's interests? This was a reminder that when a son was twelve, he moved from the mother's aegis to the father's in order to learn his trade or "business". Our Lord's first recorded words expressed absolute commitment to His Father's plan of salvation for us all.

Jesus' stay in the city and explanation to Mary and Joseph is understandable in the context of his other visits to Jerusalem. On the occasions of His Circumcision and Presentation, others spoke for Him about His identity and mission, but now He is able to make a personal statement that God's claims supercede all other considerations, even family relationships. The day would come when, on a final visit to Jerusalem with His Mother and disciples to celebrate the Passover, the Son would disclose His relationship to His Father and, again, be lost to them for three days before rising from the dead. (*cf. Lk 2:41-50*).

The Hidden Life

For the time being, the veil descends on Jesus' early years. He went home and was obedient to His parents who kept the memories and implications of these events in their hearts. The good doctor, St Luke, mentions how He grew to physical maturity, advancing in wisdom with God's blessing, and winning the golden opinions of all who knew Him. His human nature was real and, like all children, He progressed through stages of development. They are consummate imitators, and the Divine Child did not exclude Himself from His parents whose experiences, influence, and qualities are revealed in His personality. When He preached His first Sermon and eulogised the poor in spirit, those who yearn for righteousness, and the pure in heart, He remembered two people who had welcomed Him with selfless love, clothed Him, and quenched His thirst. He urged His disciples to call God "Abba", the intimate appeal of a confident child to an indulgent father, and a sound His infant lips had first relished on Mary's knee as she pointed to Joseph.

Like any other mother, Mary undertook much of Jesus' early education, and introduced Him to personal and domestic routines, skills and practices. Joseph trained the world's Creator to be a carpenter so that He could follow in his footsteps, earn a living, and contribute to the family income. (*cf. Mt 13:55; Mk 6:3*). Both parents taught their Son to love the Law and the Scriptures, and to pray the Psalms with which Mary's 'Magnificat' illustrates such detailed familiarity. (*cf. Lk 1:46-56*).

The death of Joseph

Another eighteen years passed before Our Lord appeared with His mother at the wedding in Cana, and the Christian Church assumes that Joseph had already died peacefully in their presence. In his Scripture Commentary, St Bede the Venerable is of the opinion that he was eventually buried in the Valley of Josaphat which is part of the Cedron Valley east of Jerusalem, and reputed to be the site of the Last Judgement. Josaphat was an ancestor of Joseph through whom the Messiah received His royal throne through Davidic descent. It seems splendidly appropriate that, if this is to be the scene of Our Lord's triumphant return in glory, His Foster-father's body should be the first to be reunited with his noble soul. (*cf. Mt 25:31*).

As she stood at the foot of the Cross, Our Lord entrusted His widowed Mother to St John who, from that moment, took care of her. In her turn, Mary became the trustee of the Church until Pentecost and, in John's person, accepted every human being as her own child, every one a brother and sister to her Son. (*Jn 18:25-27*).

THE CIRCUMCISION OF THE LORD

Once a Holy Day of Obligation on January 1st

Origins and significance

The early liturgies gave pride of place to the Octave of the Nativity, but there is a reference to the celebration of the Feast of the Circumcision on January 1st in the annals of the Council of Tours, 567AD. The ancient sacramentaries included exhortations to avoid the excesses of New Year celebrations, but even in the tenth century one bishop found it necessary to rebuke "those who indulge in pagan practices, songs, and lighting lamps!" The Mass and Office composed for the Feast were characterised by praise of the Blessed Virgin Mary, her privileges, and her unique contribution in the Redemption as Mother of the Saviour. The collect, a luminous example of how the liturgy transmits faith and doctrine, reads "God who hast bestowed upon mankind, through Blessed Mary's virgin motherhood, the prize of eternal salvation, grant, we pray thee, that we may feel the power of her intercession, through whom we have been privileged to welcome the giver of life, Jesus Christ, thy Son, Our Lord who is God living and reigning with you and the Holy Spirit." The Psalms and vespers were those of Mary's feasts and she was the subject of the antiphons and hymn in the office of Lauds. When the Liturgy and its Calendar were revised after the Second vatican Council, it came as no surprise when January 1st became the Solemnity of Mary, Mother of God.

After the fall of Adam and Eve, God promised them that there would be salvation for the entire human race which succeeded them. He repeated this Covenant to Noah after the Flood and told him it would last until the end of time. He enlarged upon His promise through Abraham whom He made "father of a multitude of nations"...in whom all would be blessed, whose descendants would live in the land of Canaan, and they would be the favoured trustees of the Covenant. As a sign of this special agreement with Abraham and his descendants, God ordained that, as soon as they were eight days old, all males should be circumcised, generation after generation. "My Covenant shall be marked on your bodies as a Covenant in perpetuity." (*cf. Gen 12:1-7; 17:9-14*).

God chose to demonstrate His love for all mankind through the people of Israel whom He freed from slavery and brought them back to the Promised Land. For them He gave Moses His Law on Mount Sinai and asked them. in return, to recognise and serve Him as the one, true and living God. He would send them the prophets to help them accept the salvation planned for all nations, and he would fully reveal His kindness by sending His own Son to establish a New and everlasting Covenant. (*cf. Ex 19:6f; Lev 12:3*).

In the Old Covenant, circumcision was a sacrament of legal observance and a sign of initiation into the service of God. It was a joyous celebration of a boy's admission to spiritual communion with Israel, and his share in God's promise to Abraham and the patriarchs. The rite symbolised an individual deed of covenant between God and the boy who, thereupon, embraced the Law with all its privileges and responsibilities.

From the Liturgy

"God's grace has been revealed and it has made salvation possible for the whole human race, and taught us that what we have to do is give up everything that does not lead to God…We must live good and religious lives here in this present world while we wait in hope for the blessing which will come with the appearing of our great God and Saviour, Jesus Christ." (*Epistle, Tt 2:11-14*).

"All the ends of the earth have seen the salvation of our God. Let every nation rejoice; the Lord has given proof of His saving powers and, remembering His love and promise to Israel, has shown His just dealings to all the nations." (*Gradual, Ps 97:3-4,2*).

"When the eighth day came, and the Child was to be circumcised, they gave him the name Jesus, the name the angel had given Him before His conception." (*Gospel, Lk 2:21*).

Reflection

A few days ago, the Saviour was born to the people of Israel. Now he presents himself as the appointed heir to the promises made to Abraham. Our Lord, the Lamb without blemish, was not subject to the Law, for all power had been given to him in Heaven and on earth. (*cf. Mt 28:18*), so he had no need of circumcision. He had, however, chosen to be born under God's Law, and to this He teaches obedience so that all justice should be fulfilled. He came to complete the Law and demonstrate that, in His human flesh, He was, indeed, a descendant of Abraham. The Son of Man is a true son of the race chosen to bring forth the Messiah, and He therefore subjected Himself to the painful rite of circumcision and received the name Jesus which means Saviour.

Contrary to artists' imaginative representation, circumcision did not take place in the Temple but in private houses. The public ceremony in the synagogue was introduced at a later date. Presumably, the Holy Family had found belated hospitality in Bethlehem once the census was over and accommodation became more available.

THE MOST HOLY NAME OF JESUS

*Formerly the Sunday between
the Circumcision and the Epiphany*

Christians invoke the Holy Name of Jesus with absolute confidence in Him who saves and who said, "If you ask the Father anything in my name, He will give it to you." Seventy-two disciples came back from their mission rejoicing in the submission of devils, and all the other wonders that had been accomplished in Jesus' name. His last words before ascending to His Father, with our human nature, are a message giving confidence to all who believe in the power of His name. In my name, they will cast out devils; they will have the gift of tongues; they will pick up snakes in their hands, and be unharmed should they drink deadly poison; they will lay their hands on the sick, who will recover. The Acts of the Apostles and the astonishing development of the Church testify to the immediate truth of His promise. (*cf. Jn 16:23; Lk 10:17; Mk 16:17-18; Acts 3:6; 4:8-12; 9:34-40*). It became a Christian habit to begin major undertakings with an invocation to the Holy Name, as when the emperor Justinian, about to revise the Roman Law in his Code of 529AD, said, "In the name of Jesus we begin our consultation."

The Liturgical Feast was established in the fifteenth century and the Office and Mass was composed by the Franciscan, Bernadine dei Basti. Until recent times it has been celebrated appropriately near that of the Circumcision when Our Lord received the Holy Name Jesus. It has been celebrated in honour of that Name which is above all other names, and in thanksgiving for what Jesus continues to do for all mankind in the great mystery of the Redemption.

St Bernard of Clairvaux (d.1153) was an ardent advocate of the devotion, as was the Dominican St Peter Martyr of Verona (d 1252), and in this period Pope Urban IV granted an indulgence to those who added "Jesus" to the end of the first part of the 'Hail Mary'. Pope Blessed Gregory X (d.1276) commissioned the Dominicans to preach devotion to the Holy Name, and dedicated altars became a feature of Dominican churches. He was, incidentally, the pope elected at the conclave in Viterbo, 1271, when the civil authorities expedited the decision of the cardinals by locking them in the papal palace, removing the roof, and threatening them with starvation! In 1274, he called the second Council of Lyons which urged the Society of the Most Holy Name to love and honour the Holy Name in reparation for the heresies of the Albigensians, and for profanities, blasphemy and false oaths which offend it. In the fifteenth century St Bernardine of Siena and his Franciscan confrere St John Capistrano (d.1456) preached the devotion tirelessly and were instrumental in the official insertion of the Holy Name in the 'Hail Mary' first in Italy and then to the universal Church.

As well as Urban IV and Gregory X, other popes have sustained Christian reverence to the Holy Name. Sixtus V (d.1590) attached indulgences to the aspiration "Praise be Jesus Christ! For evermore, Amen!" and to the pious pronunciation of the Holy Name, and Benedict XIII (d.1730) a plenary indulgence to this latter in the hour of death. Pope St Pius X (d. 1904) granted an indulgence of three hundred days to the invocation of the names 'Jesus and Mary' and Pope John Paul II often opens greetings with "Praised be Jesus Christ".

From the Liturgy

"His state was divine, yet He did not cling to His equality with God but emptied himself to assume the condition of a slave and became as men are; and being as all men are, He was humbler yet, even to accepting death, death on a cross. But God raised Him high and gave Him the name which is above all other names, so that all beings, in the heavens, on earth, and in the underworld should bend the knee at the name of Jesus, and every tongue should proclaim Jesus Christ as Lord to the glory of God the Father." (*Introit, Ph 2:6-11*).

"God, who appointed your only-begotten Son to be the Saviour of mankind, and asked that He should be called Jesus, grant us the grace to enjoy in Heaven the vision of Him whose Holy Name we venerate on earth." (*Collect*).

After Peter and John had cured a lame man in the name of the Lord (*Acts 3:1-10*), Peter, in the face of hostile interrogation from rulers of the people and the elders, was filled with the Holy Spirit and answered, "If you are questioning us today about an act of kindness to a cripple, and asking us how he was healed, then I am glad to tell you all, and would indeed be glad to tell the whole people of Israel, that it was by the name of Jesus Christ the Nazarene, by His name and no other, that this man is able to stand up perfectly healthy, here in your presence today...for of all names in the world given to man, this is the only one by which we can be saved." (*Lesson, Acts 4:8-12*)

"When the eighth day came and the Child was to be circumcised, they gave Him the name Jesus." (*Gospel Lk 2:21*)

Reflection

The Liturgy of the Annunciation recalls that the virginal mother was told that her child should be called Emmanuel, and that Mary was told by Gabriel that the baby she was to conceive must be called Jesus. (*Isaiah 7:14; Lk 1:32*). As soon as Joseph was made aware of God's intentions, and his own participation in the divine plan of redemption as guardian on earth of the Saviour, he assumed responsibility for naming the Child. Jewish Law prescribed that family membership was established not by biological descent but by recognition of legitimate parentage, including that by way of adoption. Joseph fulfilled the paternal, legal responsibility of giving Our Lord His name, and, though not in a biological sense, was a father to Him and His fatherhood closest to God's own. God is faithful to His promises and, to accomplish His royal and messianic mission, the Saviour is born of the House and family of David, as His genealogy through Joseph clearly shows. (*cf. Mt 1:1-25*).

Hymn in honour of the Holy Name
(From 'Jesu Rex Admirabilis' 12th Century)
"O Jesus, King most wonderful,
    Thou conqueror renowned!
Thou sweetness most ineffable in whom
    all joys are found…
May every heart confess Thy name,
    and ever Thee adore,
And, seeking Thee, itself inflame
    to seek Thee more and more.
Thee may our tongues for ever bless,
    Thee may we love alone,
And ever in our lives express the image of Thy own."

THE EPIPHANY OF THE LORD

January 6th

"On this day, Lord God, by a guiding star you revealed your only-begotten son to all the peoples of the world. Lead us from the faith by which we know you now to the vision of your glory face to face." (*Opening Prayer*).

The Feast of the Epiphany was first celebrated in the Eastern Church. It embraced revelations and manifestations of Our Lord's glory like His Baptism, the miraculous transformation of water into wine at Cana, the Nativity, and the visit of the Magi. St Gregory Nazianzen preached a sermon on December 25th, 380, in which he referred to the Nativity and looked forward to Our Lord's Baptism very shortly. Twelve days later, on January 6th, he said that as the Nativity and the coming of the Magi had already been celebrated, the commemoration of the Lord's Baptism would now take place. One of the earliest Magnificat Antiphons for January 6th reads, "We keep our holy day adorned with three miracles. Today a star led the Magi to the crib, today wine was made from water at the marriage; today, in the Jordan Christ willed to be baptised by John." The present, revised Roman Calendar preserves the association in which the Baptism of the Lord follows the Epiphany.

As time passed, December 25th became widely accepted as the date when the Nativity was celebrated. This resulted in an acknowledgement of January 6th as the Feast of Our Lord's revealing Himself to the Magi who represent all who come to believe in Him throughout time and from all corners of the earth. "It means that the pagans now share the same inheritance, that they are parts of the same body, and that the same promise has been made to them, in Christ Jesus, through the Gospel." (*Ep 3:5-6*).

From the Liturgy

"The Kings of Tarshish and the sea coasts shall pay Him tribute. The Kings of Sheba and Seba shall bring Him gifts. Before Him all kings shall fall prostrate. Every tribe shall be blessed in Him." (*Responsorial Psalm 71*).

"Arise, shine out Jerusalem, for your light has come, the glory of the Lord is rising on you, though night still covers the earth and darkness the peoples. Above you the Lord now rises and above you His glory appears. The nations come to your light and kings to your dawning brightness…the wealth of the nations comes to you; everyone in Sheba will come bringing gold, and incense, and singing the praise of the Lord." (*First Reading, Isaiah 60:1-6*).

Isaiah's prophecy, which echoes the psalmist and anticipates Simeon's '*Nunc dimittis*' (*cf. Lk 2:22-40*), was written just after the return from the Babylonian Exile about 538BC. Although the days of slavery which had been endured have now passed, there is no hint of tribal triumphalism. God's city of Jerusalem is everyone's home, just as the Church, the city of God, is where all find salvation.

The Gospel according to Matthew records the coming of the Magi (*Mt 2:1-12*).

Herod the Great still ruled in Judaea when three wise men from the East arrived in Jerusalem and enquired where they might find the new-born King of the Jews They had discovered His star which had guided them on their long journey to do Him homage. 'Magi' (Gk. 'Magor') meant a wise person who interpreted dreams, or an astrologer who understood the significance of signs which appeared in the heavens. The three who visited Our Lord probably came from Arabia, Mesopotamia, or Babylon, and they are first identified as kings by Tertullian (d.225), though he may have based his supposition on Isaiah's prophecy and David's psalm mentioned above. Traditionally their names are Caspar, Melchior, and Balthasar, and Cologne Cathedral claims to house their relics. The magi connotation does not mean that they were magicians or conjuring tricksters like those who attempted witchcraft to summon mosquitoes, or like the sorcerer Simon Magus. (*cf. Ex 8:12-15; Acts 8:9-25*).

Herod and his subjects in Jerusalem were taken aback by the Magi's arrival and their request for directions. When the king consulted the chief priests and scribes, he found little comfort in their confirmation of Micah's prophecy that a leader, to be born in Bethlehem, would be a true Shepherd to the kingdom of Israel, a title which indicated royal authority and responsibility. Herod asked his visitors to go to Bethlehem, find the Child, and call on their way back so that they could tell him where he might go and pay his own respects. As soon as they left him, the star reappeared and guided them to Jesus whom they were overjoyed to worship. They acknowledged the Son of God become Man with their gifts: gold for a King whose realm is of justice and peace, the frankincense of sacrifice for a Priest who sanctifies the people and restores them to His Father, and bitter myrrh for the Victim who immolates Himself upon the altar of the Cross to draw all things to Himself... Before the Magi left Bethlehem, the Angel (was it Gabriel again?) advised them, as they slept, to avoid Herod by circumventing Jerusalem on their return journey,

Although the Church celebrates Our Lord's revelation to the Gentile world, personified by the Magi, on January 6th it is possible that they visited Him after His being presented in the Temple, perhaps by as much as a year. Had Joseph been told to take His Family to Egypt before the Presentation, he would not have endangered Jesus by taking Him to the Temple in the city where Herod held court. Matthew also states that the Magi entered "the house" so, presumably, Joseph had found more acceptable accommodation in Bethlehem between the Nativity and the escape to Egypt. This would have facilitated the Circumcision and Presentation and avoid extra journeys to and from Nazareth. (*cf. Mt 2:12-23*).

Reflection

"Father, today you revealed in Christ your eternal plan of salvation and showed Him as the Light of all peoples. Now that His glory has shone among us, you have revealed humanity in His immortal image." (*from the Preface of the Epiphany*).

St Matthew, a Jew writing mainly for Jewish converts, is the only evangelist who relates the coming of the Magi, and, appropriately, presents Our Lord as Messiah and King. There is, however, the underlying warning that human nature can react badly if power is challenged, and Herod's massacre of the Innocents brings the account of the wise men's visit to a sad conclusion. Matthew's audience would have remembered how Pharaoh had hunted the infant Moses who, like Our Lord, was born to bring freedom to captives. While the Gentiles pay homage with their gifts and worship the new-born King, Herod, the king of the chosen people wants to kill Him. There is an echo here of how Balaam, a pagan prophet and forerunner of the Magi was ordered by Balek, king of the Moabites, to curse Israel but, inspired by God, he blessed them instead. The wisdom and faith of the Magi enables them to see in a baby the Star who unites divinity with humanity, and time with eternity.

"This is the day of which David sang 'All the nations you have made shall come and worship you Lord, and glorify your name,' and again, 'The Lord has made His salvation known; in the sight of the nations He has revealed His justice. This, indeed, we know to be taking place ever since the three Magi were called from their far-off land and were led by the star to worship and recognise the King of Heaven and earth, and surely their worship of Him exhorts us to imitation; that, as far as we can, we should be at the service of this grace which invites all men to Christ." (*Office of readings, St Leo the Great*).

THE PRESENTATION OF THE LORD

February 2nd

Origins and significance

The Lord spoke to Moses "Consecrate all the first born to me, the first issue of every womb among the sons of Israel…If a woman conceives and gives birth to a boy, she is to be unclean for seven days. On the eighth day, the child's foreskin must be circumcised and she must wait another thirty-three days for her blood to be purified. Then she is to bring to the priest, at the entrance to the Tent of Meeting, a lamb, one year old, for a holocaust, and a young pigeon or turtle-dove as a sacrifice for sin. If she cannot offer a lamb, she is to take two turtle doves or two young pigeons, one for the holocaust, and the other for the sacrifice for sin. The priest is to perform the rite of atonement over her and she will be purified." (*Ex 13:2; Lv 12:2-8*).

The Feast, first celebrated by the early Church at Jerusalem, marks Our Lord's entrance into His Father's House and service, and was referred to simply as the "Fortieth day after Epiphany", hardly surprising since the Nativity and the Epiphany were commemorated on the same day (*Nativity*). Once the date for the Nativity had been fixed on December 25th, the feast on the fortieth day was observed with greater solemnity on February 2nd. In the East it was always a feast of Our Lord but, from the seventh century, the West called it Candlemas or the Purification of the Blessed Virgin Mary, and so it remained until the revised Calendar of 1969 restored the title and emphasis of "The Presentation of the Lord".

From the eleventh century, candles have been blessed as a sign that the Christmas Festival is concluded, and are carried alight in procession to recall the entry of Our Lord, the Light of the World, into His Temple. It is a foretaste of the heavenly Jerusalem and His arrival in human hearts. "O gates lift up your heads; grow higher ancient doors. Let Him enter, the King of Glory." (*Ps 23*).

Pope Paul VI describes the Feast as a joint celebration of Son and Mother in the accomplishment of salvation, and Pope John Paul II as a symbol of life's dedication to reproduce Our Lord's characteristics in the Church and the world. As a candle illuminates the surrounding dark, so one's calling, be it to the priesthood, religious or family life, can radiate the Light of Christ to the world. The Holy Spirit is not constrained by human imperfections which, therefore, need not be a barrier or deterrent to personal commitment.

From the Liturgy

"The Lord God says, 'Look, I am going to send my messenger to prepare a way before me, and the Lord you are seeking will suddenly enter His Temple, and the Angel of the Covenant for whom you long, yes, he is coming…He will purify the sons of Levi, and then they will make the offering to the Lord as it should be made. The offering of Judah and Jerusalem will then be welcomed by the Lord as in former days, as in the days of old.'" (*First Reading, Ml 3:1-4*).

"Since all the children share the same blood and flesh, Jesus too shared equally in it, so that by His death He could take away all the power the Devil had over death, and set free all who had been held in slavery all their lives by the fear of death. For it was not the angels that He took to Himself; He took to Himself descent from Abraham. It was essential that He should, in this way, become completely like His brethren, so that He could become a compassionate and trustworthy High Priest able to atone for human sins. Because He has Himself been through temptation, He is able to help others who are tempted." (*Second Reading, Heb 2:14-18*).

Reflection

The Lord's coming, as the prophet Malachi suggests, could be sudden and unexpected but, in His kindness, He sends His messenger, John the Baptist, to preach repentance for the forgiveness of sin. This is to prepare a path for Him so that human hearts will be alert to His arrival. The sons of Levi who were the priests ordained to teach God's Law, and offer sacrifice with honourable fidelity, had allowed human frailty to stifle their devotion. The Lord comes to restore this priesthood so that a sacrifice is offered which is, once more, pleasing and acceptable. God Himself is the Angel who establishes the New Covenant and St Paul tells the Hebrews that He did not come to help immortal angels, but mortal men and women represented by Abraham's race to which He chose to belong, as God had promised. A new sacerdotal ministry is introduced by the perfect and compassionate High Priest, the Lamb of God who sacrifices Himself upon the altar of the Cross to expiate the sins of His people.

The time had come for the Law of purification to be observed, and for God to meet His people. Mary and Joseph took Jesus to the Temple to present Him to God and redeem him by making the offering of the poor which was a pair of turtle-doves or two young pigeons. (*cf,.Ex 13:2; Lv 12:6-8; Nb 18:15*). Israel's Saviour came as God's delegate and heir to the promises made by the prophets. His first visit to the Temple was not marked by ceremonial pomp. There was nothing to distinguish the Holy Family from all the other worshippers, but the prophecies are fulfilled and the rituals confirm that the Lord is one with His people in their humanity. Appropriately, He was greeted by Simeon, a pious priest and a worthy son of Levi who was a strict observer of the Law. He had been inspired to visit the Temple that very day and was keeping prayerful watch with a devout, elderly prophetess called Anna.

In both Old and New Covenants, prophecy is more a declaration of things known by God's revelation than a prediction of the future. By worldly standards, Simeon and Anna are not very important, yet they are chosen to welcome the Messiah and throw light on His future, about which His parents were still unsure.

A life-time of prayer enabled Simeon to see the Child as the hoped-for Messiah who would restore Israel's fortunes and bring the light of revelation to all the nations. He could depart this life in peace, having announced Our Lord's mission, though it might not be a populist triumph and, indeed, a painful sword of suffering would pierce His Mother's heart. Anna joined Simeon in thanking God for the liberation of Sion from Satan's influence. The Shepherds, the Magi, and now Simeon and Anna, stand for all embraced within God's Kingdom, and demonstrate that faith and a receptive heart outshine status when it comes to acknowledging the Saviour. Having fulfilled their religious obligations, Mary and Joseph take Jesus home to Galilee still in awe at their reception in the Temple, and pondering on everything they had experienced. (*cf. Lk 2:22-40*)

THE BAPTISM OF THE LORD

Sunday after the Epiphany

Origins and significance

The Jewish people were familiar with baptism because it was used to admit Gentiles to Judaism, and the Essenes conducted ritual washings to signify commitment to moral and religious purity. John the Baptist called the people to put their lives in order so that they should be suitably prepared for the coming of the Messiah, and to show their firm purpose by being cleansed in the waters of the Jordan. He explained that his baptism was a preparation for the Baptism in the Holy Spirit which the Messiah would bring. The limitations of the Jewish ceremonial bath to wash away gentile "defilement" would give way to the efficacious, sacramental rebirth in Our Lord's Baptism, and a sublimation of the Old Law in the arrival of the New Covenant. Through such a Baptism flow all the gifts of grace, and not only in the Sacrament but in the entire economy of salvation.

After John had been preaching and baptising for about six months, he sensed that he was attracting more veneration than was his due. He told his followers that he baptised only with water but One was coming to baptise in the Holy Spirit, and He was of such worth that he did not deserve to perform the most menial task of untying His sandals. (*cf. Mk 1:7-11; Lk 3:15-16*).

From the Liturgy

"Almighty, eternal God, when the spirit descended upon Jesus at His baptism in the Jordan, you revealed Him as your own beloved Son. Keep us, your children born of water and the Spirit, faithful to our calling." (*Opening Prayer*).

"Jesus came from Galilee to the Jordan to be baptised by John. John tried to dissuade Him. 'It is I who need baptism from you', he said 'and yet you come to me!' But Jesus replied, 'Leave it like this for the time being; it is fitting that we should, in this way, do all that righteousness demands.' At this, John gave in to Him. As soon as Jesus was baptised He came up from the water, and suddenly the heavens opened and He saw the Spirit of God descending like a dove and coming down on Him. And a voice spoke from heaven, 'This is my Son, the Beloved; my favour rests on Him.'" (*Gospel, Mt 3:13-17*).

Reflection

Our Lord was thirty years old when He left Nazareth to begin His public life and travel south to the district which bordered the Jordan to meet John and present Himself for baptism. The Gospel has told us of John's reticence and Jesus' reassurance that all should be accomplished in the cause of righteousness.

Jeremiah had promised that a Righteous Branch would issue from the House of David, and his prophecy is fulfilled in Christ, the Sun of Righteousness, whose dawning light dispels the darkness of sin and the shadows of death. He brings Justice, not as an enforcer, but as a Servant and Shepherd-King who transforms hearts in the way that a branch encourages new life.

John did not baptise without giving prior instruction but, in Jesus' case, he recognised the Teacher without compare. Given the family love manifested by Mary's visit to Elizabeth (*cf. Lk 1:39-56*), the two men must have known each other, and Matthew's Gospel indicates that there had been earlier conversations which had helped John form an opinion... He certainly understood Jesus' wish to identify Himself with the repentant sinners who would become His disciples, and in whose lives He wished to be totally involved.

Our Lord's baptism of water is followed by Baptism of the Holy Spirit, the Dove who brooded on the face of the waters in the first creation. Now he rests on Jesus while the Father, the voice of creation in the beginning, claims His beloved Son whose mission He invests with Messianic dignity. Jesus gives John's mission ultimate approval by submitting to his baptism and now He initiates His own as God's suffering Servant. He is sinless and has no need of cleansing, but He associates Himself with the members of His Mystical Body to show that the baptism of death brings a new birth of reconciliation with the Father. Afterwards, the Spirit leads Him to the desert where he fasts for forty days and nights. He has no need of penance, but He sets an example, and gives Satan notice that the battle has been joined. (*cf. Mt 3:13-17; Mk 1:9-11*). When the obedient Abraham was willing to sacrifice Isaac, the cherished, only son of his old age, the boy innocently asked where was the lamb for the oblation. His father told him that God would provide. When God was about to free His people from Egyptian slavery, He ordered that a spotless, male lamb should be offered. In consuming it, the Hebrews accepted His merciful deliverance, and the blood of the lamb on their doorposts saved them from the avenging angel. When Isaiah foretold the coming of God's chosen, Suffering Servant, he saw Him as one who would "be led out like a lamb for the slaughter."

As soon as John the Baptist heard the voice of the Father presenting His beloved Son, He knew that Jesus was the expected Messiah, and that his mission as prophetic herald was almost at an end. Surrounded by his own disciples, he pointed to Jesus and announced Him as "the Lamb of God who takes away the sins of the world." In this expression of sacred significance, all the Old Testament images completely come together. Jesus is the sacrificial Paschal Lamb without blemish who is offered to expiate sin and, in the Eucharist, gives His flesh and blood for our spiritual food and drink. As He did for Abraham and Isaac, God provides the sacrifice and, in his identification, John foretells Our Lord's death and the end of the Judaic sacrificial ritual.

Everything promised by God through His prophets has come to pass, and the last prophet actually sees the Lamb who redeems with His blood. In obedience to His Father's will the innocent Lamb has accepted John's baptism and, with it, the baptism of death which saves the world from the result of sin. He will be sacrificed at the very hour when, according to Mosaic law, the lambs for the Passover sacrifice should be killed in the Temple. Like these sacrificial lambs, not one of His bones will be broken. Our Lord, however, is the triumphant Lamb who, like His ancestor David, defeats all beasts and reptiles and is the heavenly Victor to whom is entrusted the future of the earth. (*cf. Jn 1:1-34; Is 53:1-7; Rv 4*).

THE TRANSFIGURATION OF THE LORD

August 6th

Origins and significance

The sermons of St Leo the Great reveal that the Feast was celebrated in Rome at least from the middle of the fifth century. In 1457, Pope Calixtus III decreed that it should be a solemnity throughout the universal Church. The fifteenth century hymn '*Caelestis formam gloriae*' is indicative of devotion.

"O wondrous type, O vision fair
    of glory that the Church shall share,
Which Christ upon the mountain shows
    where brighter than the sun He glows;
The law and prophets there have place
    as chosen witnesses of grace;
The Father's voice from out the cloud
    proclaims His only Son aloud.

With shining face and bright array,
    Christ deigns to manifest today
What glory shall to faith be given
    when we enjoy our God in Heaven;
And Christian hearts are raised on high

> by that great vision's mystery
> For which, in thankful strains, we raise
> on this glad day the voice of praise."

From the Liturgy

"God our Father, in the transfigured glory of Christ your Son, you strengthen our faith by confirming the witness of your prophets, and show us the splendour of your beloved sons and daughters. As we listen to the voice of your Son, help us to become heirs to eternal life with Him for he lives and reigns with you and the Holy Spirit, one God, for ever and ever." (*Opening Prayer*).

In his second letter, St Peter writes, "It was not any cleverly invented myths that we were repeating when we brought you the knowledge of the power and the coming of our Lord Jesus Christ; we had seen His majesty for ourselves. He was honoured and glorified by God the Father, when the sublime glory itself spoke to Him and said, "This is my Son, the beloved; He enjoys my favour." We heard this ourselves, spoken from heaven, when we were with him on the holy mountain. So we have confirmation of what was said in prophecies; and you will be right to depend on prophecy and take it as a lamp for lighting a way through the dark until the dawn comes and the morning star rises in your minds." (*Second Reading, 2 P 1:16-19*).

The three synoptic Gospels record the Transfiguration (*Mt 17:1-9; Mk 9:2-10; Lk 9:28-36*).

Reflection

Our Lord and His disciples had spent time visiting the villages near the city of Caesarea Philippi built by Philip the Tetrarch on the site of an ancient sanctuary dedicated to Pan. He had been very careful not to draw too much official attention to Himself but now, in this pagan place, He felt he could discuss the question of his identity with the disciples, and He asked them what people were saying about Him. They told Him about the rumours which were circulating in Herod's court that he was John the Baptist who had come back from the dead, or perhaps Elijah himself, or some other prophet like one of those who regularly introduced themselves to society. Some of the people hoped he might be the Messiah, but were disappointed that He had not fulfilled their expectations of a conquering hero. Our Lord asked the disciples for their own opinion and Peter, with characteristic spontaneity, declared, "You are the Christ, the Son of the Living God."

Six days after this profession of faith, Our Lord took Peter, James and John to Mount Tabor, about two days walk away but familiar territory because it was only a few miles from Nazareth. After the appointment of the Apostles (*Lk 6:12-16*), the trio had become an inner circle who had already witnessed the revival of Jairus' daughter (*Mk 5:21-43*) and, in about twelve months time, would accompany Him to the Garden of Gethsemane just before His arrest. (*Mt 26:36-46*). Now, on the heights of Tabor, they witnessed His glorious divinity shine forth in luminous majesty as head of redeemed humanity and Lord of all creation. They watched Him in conversation with Moses and Elijah, the old dispensation of the Law and the Prophets, side by side with the authentic source of divine Truth who brings a New Covenant. Peter thought that such a wonderful transfiguration must be the inauguration of a victorious Messianic reign, and that Moses and Elijah had returned to earth to enjoy the triumph. In his euphoria, he said it was a good thing that James, John and himself were on hand because they could improvise three shelters for His master and the two visitors, from the trees which crowned Tabor. It was not a feasible suggestion and, in any case, Moses, Elijah and Our Lord did not need earthly dwellings, but it did pave the way for a further revelation about the Trinity.

When Our Lord was baptised in the Jordan, the Holy Spirit had appeared as a dove, and the Father had announced, "You are my beloved Son in whom I am well pleased." Now, at the Transfiguration, the cloud of divine presence enveloped the three Apostles, and they heard the Father's voice confirming what Peter had attested at Caesare Philippi. "This is my beloved Son. Listen to all He says." The Father loves the Son whose words must be heeded; the Son loves the Father who wills Redemption; the Spirit, who proceeds from their love, reveals the Son who restores humanity to the

Trinity. The vision passes and Jesus is, once more, their familiar Master and friend.

The Transfiguration of Our Lord, with the appearance of Moses and Elijah, and the declaration of the Father, was a confirmation of everything He had taught the Apostles about His own person and His relation to the Old Law. It was also to strengthen their faith and prepare them for the trials of His Passion and, eventually, their own sufferings and death. He told them to say nothing about what they had seen until after the Resurrection. Knowledge of the Transfiguration might have led to misinterpretation, inappropriate Messianic enthusiasm, and obscured the necessity of the Cross.

"He revealed His glory to the disciples to strengthen them for the scandal of the Cross. His glory shone from a body like our own, to show that the Church, which is the Body of Christ, would one day share his glory." (*Preface*).

THE BODY AND BLOOD OF CHRIST

Thursday after Trinity Sunday

Origins and significance

The solemn celebration of the Feast of Corpus Christi began in the diocese of Liège in 1246, following the revelations of the French nun, Juliana of Cornillon (d.1258). After enthusiastic emulation throughout Europe, it was promulgated to the universal Church by Pope Urban IV in 1264. The liturgy, in the composition of which St Thomas Aquinas was so eminently instrumental, duplicated the Eucharistic focus of Holy Thursday and highlighted the redemptive effects of the Sacrament. Since the fourteenth century, a characteristic of the ensuing and heartfelt devotion has been the Eucharistic procession of the Blessed Sacrament in which the consecrated Host is carried in a monstrance.

Our Old Testament ancestors associated blood more with a perception of the entire human being than with the fluid which courses through its veins and, in the New Covenant, this inspired devotion to the Precious Blood of Our Lord who gave His last drop upon the Cross. In 1849, Pope Pius IX nominated the first Sunday in July as the Feast of the Precious Blood and, in 1960, Pope John

XXIII approved the Litany of the Precious Blood. The Second Vatican Council looked to the whole person of Our Lord and, from 1970, the Feasts of Corpus Christi and the Precious Blood became the unified Solemnity of the Body and Blood of Christ.

On Holy Thursday Our Lord fulfilled His wish to eat the Passover with His disciples, and during the meal he gave them the Eucharist. The words 'bread' and 'wine' were given a new and transformed meaning which predicted and enacted His gift of Self. The following day, He gave His Body and Blood on Calvary and instituted an everlasting oblation for humanity.

The Passover meal celebrated God's liberation of His people, the continuing covenant with them, and prefigures Our Lord's liberation of the world from sin through His death. His prayer at the Last Supper is influenced by Jewish heritage in the bread and cup of religious meals, accompanied by blessing and thanksgiving to God for His mercies. The meals He shared are also significant in the Judaic tradition in which the reign of God at the end of time is seen as a festive meal, an image He continued in His parables and actions. The meals Our Lord shared with social outcasts, and for which He was criticised, were manifestations of God's mercy and reign which excludes no one. The Last Supper is within the context of meals of reconciliation with sinners in His public life, and with His disciples after His Resurrection.

St Thomas Aquinas developed the philosophical insights of Aristotle and St Augustine to explain that the bread and wine can be changed substantially into the real presence of Christ, while the "accidents" like colour, taste, and shape are unaltered. He insisted, however that the mystery of the Eucharist, observable to the eyes of faith, remains beyond theological explanation, and taught that when the priest, acting "in the person of Christ" consecrates the bread and wine with the words of Christ, it is Christ Himself who is effecting the transubstantiation, a term which the Fourth Lateran Council had introduced in 1215. The Council of Trent (1545-63) reaffirmed the real, true and substantial presence of Christ under the appearance of bread and wine after the consecration at Mass.

From the Liturgy

"Lord, you gave us the Eucharist as the memorial of your suffering and death. May our worship of this sacrament of your Body and Blood help us to experience the salvation you have won for us and the peace of the Kingdom where you live with the Father and the Holy Spirit, one God, forever." (*Opening Prayer*).

"Melchizedek king of Salem brought bread and wine; he was a priest of God Most High. He pronounced this blessing: 'Blessed be Abraham By God Most High, creator of heaven and earth, and blessed be God Most High for handing over your enemies to you." (*Gn 14:18-20*).

"The blessing-cup that we bless is a communion with the blood of Christ, and the bread that we break is a communion with the body of Christ. The fact that there is only one loaf means that, though there are many of us, we form a single body because we all have a share in this one loaf." (*1Co 10:16-17*).

"He took bread, and thanked God for it and broke it, and He said, 'This is my body which is for you; do this as a memorial of me.' In the same way He took the cup after supper, and said, 'This cup is the new covenant in my blood. Whenever you drink it, do this as a memorial of me." (*1Co 11:23-26*).

Jesus said, "I am the living bread which has come down from heaven. Anyone who eats this bread will live for ever…Anyone who eats my flesh and drinks my blood has eternal life, and I shall raise him up on the last day…He who eats my flesh and drinks my blood lives in me and I live in him. As I, who am sent by the living Father, myself draw life from the Father, so whoever eats me will draw life from me…anyone who eats this bread will live for ever. " (*Jn 6:51-58*).

Reflection

There can be no better summary of the wonders of this Feast and the Sacrament of the Eucharist than the words of St Thomas Aquinas which the Church remembers in the Office of Readings.

The Body and Blood of Christ

"The only-begotten Son of God, wishing to enable our share in His divinity, assumed our nature so that, by becoming man, He might make men gods. The nature He assumed He turned to our salvation, for He offered His body to God the Father on the altar of the cross for our reconciliation, and He shed His blood for our ransom and cleansing so that we might be redeemed from wretched captivity and cleansed from all sins.

In order that we might preserve the memory of this great act of love, He left His body as food and His blood as drink, to be received by the faithful under the appearances of bread and wine. At this meal, Christ the true God is set before us to eat. This sacrament purges away our sins, increases our virtues, and nourishes our minds with an abundance of all the spiritual gifts. The sweetness of the Spirit is tasted at its source and the memory is celebrated of that surpassing love which Christ showed in His Passion.

And so, to imprint the immensity of this love more deeply in the hearts of the faithful, at the Last Supper, when the Lord had celebrated the Pasch with His disciples and was about to pass from this world to His Father, He instituted this sacrament as a perpetual memorial of His Passion. It fulfilled the type of the Old Law, was the the greatest of the miracles He worked, and He left it as a unique consolation for those who were desolate at his departure."

THE RESURRECTION

Origins and significance

In 325AD, the Council of Nicaea decreed that the Feast of Our Lord's Resurrection, the most important Christian celebration, should be on the Sunday following the full moon of the Spring Equinox between March 22nd and April 25th. The date of Easter determines, therefore, the timing of movable feasts like the Ascension, the Most Holy Trinity, and the number of weeks prior to Lent and after Pentecost. The Easter Season, beginning with its Octave, lasts fifty days until Pentecost during which period the Paschal Candle, blessed at the Easter Vigil, is lit during Mass, and the water, similarly sanctified, is used for Baptism.

The Judaic Passover united the separate festivals of the spring sacrifice of nomadic shepherds and of Unleavened Bread adopted by the Hebrews after settling in Canaan. In the first century, as today, the Passover feast recalled Israel's liberation from slavery and humanity's abiding hope of redemption, and is the context of the Last Supper and the events leading to Our Lord's crucifixion and Resurrection. By the second century, the Church was celebrating a Christian Passover, or 'Pascha', a feast of memory and hope in Jesus, the Paschal Lamb of the New

Covenant, with thanksgiving for deliverance from sin and death, and joyful expectation of everlasting life. This early Pascha also remembered Our Lord's Passion and Death, and included the celebration of His Incarnation, Ascension and glorification as King of heaven and earth, and the total work of Redemption epitomised in His Cross as the symbol of victory. The liturgy for the three day period of preparation commemorated the events of the Passion at various "stations" in Jerusalem which was a major destination for pilgrims, and on Good Friday, for example, the Cross was venerated for the three hours of Our Lord's agony. The churches of Constantinople and Rome adopted these services during the fifth and sixth centuries, but the mediaeval West lost sight of the link between the Holy Week liturgies and their original times and places. Pope Pius XII sought to remedy this by the restoration of the Easter Triduum, a development continued by the Second Vatican Council. In God's eternal present moment, Easter is more than a series of Gospel recollections. It is the continued passage of His people in Christ through death to a new life.

The Easter Vigil

This second century nocturnal watch, the third part of the Triduum of Our Lord's Passion, Resurrection, and Victory over death, is one of the oldest Christians celebrations. St Augustine described it as "the mother of all vigils, the high point of the Church's year, the encapsulation of the Paschal mystery, and a rehearsal of salvation history in word and song." It became the time when the newly baptised representing the Risen Lord are initiated, and when the blessing of the new fire and paschal candle proclaim the Light of Christ in the 'Exultet'. A new life is the theme of seven Old Testament readings in the Liturgy, one of which recounts Abraham's willingness to sacrifice Isaac, the prefigurement of Our Lord's perfect sacrifice. We die with Him in Baptism to share the new life He brings in the Resurrection, and, during our mortal lives, the Risen Lord nourishes us with His own body and Blood in the Eucharist. "Father, we praise you with joy when Christ became our Paschal Sacrifice. He is the true Lamb who takes away the sins of the world. By dying He destroyed our death; by rising He restored our life." (*Preface of Easter*)

From the Liturgy of Easter Sunday

Peter addressed Cornelius and his household. "They killed Him by hanging Him on a tree, yet three days afterwards God raised Him to life and allowed Him to be seen, not by the whole people but only by certain witnesses God had chosen beforehand. Now we are those witnesses; we have eaten and drunk with Him after His resurrection, and he has ordered us to proclaim this to His people, and to tell them that God has appointed Him to judge everyone alive or dead...All who believe in Jesus will have their sins forgiven through His name." (*First Reading, Acts 10:37-43*).

"Since you have been brought back to true life in Christ, you must look for the things that are in heaven where Christ is sitting at God's right hand. Let your thoughts be on heavenly things, not on things that are on the earth, because you have died and now the life you have is hidden with Christ in God. But when Christ is revealed – and he is your life – you too will be revealed in all your glory with Him…Christ our Passover has been sacrificed; let us celebrate the feast by getting rid of the old yeast of evil and wickedness, having only the unleavened bread of sincerity and truth." (*Second Readings, Col 3:1-4; 1 Co 5:6-8*).

Reflection

Cornelius was one of the Roman centurions stationed in Palestine whom the New testament presents in a favourable light. (*cf. Mt 8:5-13*). Though not yet a Gentile convert, He devoutly worshipped God, supported Jewish interests, and, with all his family and servants, was baptised by St Peter when he visited his house in Caesarea. He would have been unaware of the Resurrection because Our Lord had appeared only to the Apostles and a few chosen disciples, but Peter makes it quite clear that now he brings news of the Resurrection and the forgiveness of sin to all the people, including the Gentiles.

St Paul teaches that we die a mystical death when we descend into the cleansing waters of Baptism, but we die only to be raised to a new life in Christ. Living involves thinking, loving and doing, so life is a raising of the heart to God until all the members of Christ's body are united to their Head in glory. He reminds us that leaven represents sin which spreads like yeast through dough, hence the Jewish practice of removing yeast from the house before Passover and, for eight days after, eating only unleavened bread.

The Gospel of Easter Sunday (cf. Jn 20:1-9).

On the Sabbath Eve, Joseph of Arimathea had not had time to embalm Our Lord's Body so, before dawn on the Sunday morning, Mary of Magdala went to the tomb in advance of the other women who were going to perform this last service. She saw that the stone was rolled back from the entrance and that the tomb was empty so ran immediately to find Peter and John, and told them the Lord was not in the tomb and she did not know where He had been taken. The two Apostles raced to the tomb, the youthful John outstripping his senior. He looked through the low opening and saw the linen cloths lying on the ground but he did not enter, waiting respectfully for Peter who went in as soon as he arrived. He was puzzled by what he saw. Body-snatchers do not carefully remove lines bands from the body before making off, but here the bandages, far from being in a confused heap, were lying where the body had been, and the napkin which had covered the head was to one side, neatly rolled up.

When John entered, the light of his faith enabled him to see the truth at once and understand the teaching of Scripture that Our Lord must rise from the dead: "So my heart exults, my very soul rejoices, my body too will rest securely, for you will not abandon my soul to Sheol, nor allow the one you love to see the Pit; you will reveal the path of life to me, give me unbounded joy in your presence and, at your right hand, everlasting pleasures." (*Ps 16:9-11*). Before He ascended to sit in glory at His Father's right hand, Our Lord told the Apostles that everything written about Him in the Law of Moses, the Prophets and the Psalms had to be fulfilled and that on the third day He would rise from the dead. (*Lk 24:44*). At Pentecost, Peter told the assembled crowd that when David wrote this Psalm, he was not speaking of himself but of the Lord whom God freed "from the pangs of Hades", an explanation later repeated by St Paul when he preached at Antioch. (*cf. Acts 2:26-33; 13:34-37*).

"We Lord, with faithful hearts and voice
    on this your rising day rejoice,
O thou whose power o'ercame the grave,
    by grace and love us sinners save."
(*Hymn, Liturgy of the Hours*).

THE ASCENSION

Thursday of the Sixth Week of Easter

Origins and significance

The Feast celebrates Our Lord's return to Heaven by His own divine power forty days after His Resurrection. There is no documentary evidence before the fifth century about its observance, but St Augustine and St John Chrysostom are convinced it is of Apostolic origin, and certainly it was an occasion precious to the Apostles who realised its full import when Pentecost produced their remarkable transformation. Our Lord's Ascension (*Mt 28:16-20; Mk 16:19-20; Lk 24:50-53; Acts 1:2*), may well have been celebrated in association with Easter and, later, Pentecost.

Certain customs became associated with the early liturgy such as the blessing of grapes after the commemoration of the dead, and there were torchlit processions with banners to honour Our Lord's regal entry into Heaven. In England, the procession was led by "Christ's Banner", a lion on the front and a dragon on the back symbolising His victory over Satan. With the Passion, Easter, and Pentecost it is one of the great ecumenical feasts observed by all Christians, and the liturgy rejoices in Our Lord's work of salvation, His return to the Godhead with human nature glorified, and the promise of our own glory to come.

From the Liturgy

"God our Father, make us joyful in the ascension of your Son, Jesus Christ. May we follow Him into the new creation, for His ascension is our glory and hope." (*Opening Prayer*).

The eleven Apostles remained in Jerusalem until the end of Paschal week and, once they were convinced that their Master was no longer vulnerable, they returned to their homes and occupations. During the next five weeks, Our Lord regularly appeared to them and told them more about the Kingdom of God. When the time approached for His departure, He said that when He was gone, they must return to Jerusalem and wait there to be baptised with the Holy Spirit as the Father had promised. In the meantime, He arranged to meet them on high ground above the Sea of Galilee, and some say that this was the site of the Sermon on the Mount in which He introduced the Kingdom. If so it was wonderfully appropriate.

Despite everything Our Lord had taught them, the Apostles still hoped for an immediate Messianic reign in Israel, no doubt with themselves in positions of influence. He patiently explained that when they received the Holy Spirit in ten days time, they would be empowered to represent Him not just in Jerusalem, Judaea and Samaria, but throughout the whole world. In an assurance of His divinity, He said He had all authority over heaven and earth, and now they were to go and make disciples of all nations, and baptise them in the name of the Trinity to which the Person of Incarnate God was about to return. They were to teach everyone to observe the precepts He had given them but, because this was no easy task, His light, and the strength of His presence would be with them and their successors until the end of time. Our Lord then ascended into Heaven and was lost to the Apostles' sight but two angels came to comfort them and His followers throughout the ages. "Jesus who has been taken from you into heaven…will come back in the same way as you have seen him go." He will come again in glory on the clouds of Heaven with His angels accompanying Him to serve His judgement. (*cf. Acts 1:1-14; Mt 24:30-31; 28:16-20*)

"God goes up with shouts of joy; the Lord goes up with trumpet blast. Sing praise for God, sing praise to our King…God is King of all the nations; God reigns on His holy throne. (*Responsorial Psalm 46*).

"May the God of Our Lord Jesus Christ enlighten the eyes of your mind so that you can see what hope His call holds for you…This you can tell from the strength of His power at work in Christ, when He used it to raise Him from the dead, and to make Him sit at His right hand in Heaven, far above every Sovereignty, Authority, Power, or Domination, or any other name that can be named, not only in this age but in the age to come. He has put all things under His feet, and made Him, as the ruler of everything, the Head of the Church which is his Body, the fullness of Him who fills the whole creation." (*Second Reading, Ep 1:17-23*)

Reflection

St Paul prays for us to receive the gift of loving faith to appreciate the blessings God has in store for humanity. Human frailty need not fear because God's power is seen in the Resurrection and Ascension wherein the Son is glorified. His dignity, exalted above all created beings, embraces the members of the Church of which He is Head, in the union of His divine and human natures. The Apostles' Creed declares belief that He ascended into Heaven and sits at the Father's right hand, a position which signifies the establishment of the Messiah's Kingdom where, in His glorified humanity, He continues to intercede for mankind. His obedience unto death has been followed by His Resurrection and, with His Ascension, comes His formal investiture as King of Heaven and earth. Such authority has always been His but now it is as the Son of Man that He takes formal possession of His throne "with dominion, and glory, and kingdom, so that all peoples, nations, and languages should serve Him; His dominion is everlasting." (*Dan 7:14*).

The Apostles had been distraught at the thought of Our Lord's leaving them but He promised that, upon His return to the Father, He would send the Holy Spirit. This Paraclete and new Advocate would stay with them forever, teach them all things, remind them of everything Jesus had said, and inspire progress to eternal life. The Holy Spirit comes to every person ever born, making present the One who has risen and ascended, never forcing, but never desisting. This is the greatest gift of the Father's love for His children, and the Son died and rose again so that they might possess it always. Through the work of the Holy spirit, the Father willed that the Son should become man so that man might be made divine and, on Ascension day, we pray with the Apostles for a new outpouring of the Holy Spirit and to be clothed with power from on high.

> "Sower and seed of man's reprieving,
>   Jesus, the longing heart's repose,
> Thine own creation's fault retrieving,
>   pure light thy lover only knows;
> What sovereign pity earthward drew thee,
>   our load of sins thy charge to make,
> Slain, that the guilty race that slew thee
>   life from thy guiltless death might take?..

(from Hymn, Liturgy of the Hours).

The Sacred Heart of Jesus

Friday after the Second Sunday after Pentecost

Origins and significance.

"The soldiers came and broke the legs of the first man who had been crucified with Him, and then the other. When they came to Jesus, they found that He was already dead, so, instead of breaking His legs, one of the soldiers pierced His side with a lance; and immediately there came out blood and water. All this happened to fulfil the words of scripture: 'Not one of his bones will be broken' and, again, in another place scripture says 'They will look on the one whom they have pierced.'" (*Jn 19:31-37; cf. Ex 13:46; Nb 9:12; Ze 12:10*).

St John's account is the biblical and historical basis for devotion to the Sacred Heart. The Jews were anxious that the bodies should be removed before the sabbath began at sunset and they asked Pilate for the legs to be broken so that death from shock would be immediate. As Our Lord had been dead for some time, John recognised that the flow of blood and water was an extraordinary phenomenon beyond physiological explanation, but the reality is not doubted. The Fathers of the Church saw the two liquids as symbols of the sacraments, especially

Baptism and the Eucharist, and these life giving streams as the graces which create the Church, the second Eve from the side of the second Adam asleep on the Cross. Our Lord promised that from His heart living water would flow, and the Church believes that it thus received the Holy Spirit. "From His pierced side blood and water flowed to pay the price of our salvation. With blood from the secret recesses of His heart came the Church's sacraments with their power to confer the life of grace, and a draught of living water welling up to eternal life." (*St Bonaventure, d.1719*).

John Eudes (d.1680), a priest of the French Oratory, composed the Office of the Sacred Heart in 1668 and, with episcopal approval, the celebration of the Feast began in the Normandy seminaries he had founded. Margaret Mary Alacoque (d.1690), a Visitation sister at Paray-le-Monial, was favoured with visions of Our Lord who asked her to kindle devotion to His Sacred Heart which symbolised His love for mankind so often sadly rejected. Her teaching and accounts of the visions, in which work she was supported by the Jesuit, Claude la Colombiere, were blessed with remarkable influence on the Church's devotional life. In 1856, Pope Gregory XVI decreed that the Feast of the Sacred Heart was to be celebrated in the universal Church, and it was inserted in the Roman calendar, initially on the Friday following the Octave of Corpus Christi. The Catechism of the Catholic Church (1437; 2669) teaches that the Church honours and venerates the Heart of Jesus, "just as it invokes the Holy Name. It adores the Incarnate Word and His Heart which, out of love for men, He allowed to be pierced for our sins. Only the Heart of Christ who knows the depths of the Father's love could reveal the abyss of His mercy in the beautiful parable of the Prodigal Son." (*cf. Lk 15:11-32*).

Pope Leo XIII declared John Eudes the author of the liturgical worship of the Sacred Heart of Jesus, and St Pius X added that he should be regarded as the father and doctor of this devotion. He and Sister Margaret Mary were canonised by Pope Benedict XV, and Claude la Colombiere by Pope John Paul II as recently as 1992.

From the Liturgy

"The thoughts of His heart last through every generation, that he will rescue them from death and feed them in time of famine." (*Entrance Antiphon*)

"Father, we have wounded the Heart of Jesus your Son, but He brings us forgiveness and grace. Help us to prove our grateful love and make amends for our sins." (*Opening Prayer*).

"I myself will pasture my sheep. I myself will show them where to rest. I shall look for the lost one, bring back the stray, bandage the wounded and make the weak strong…I shall be a true shepherd to them." (*First Reading, Ez 34:11-16*).

"It is he who forgives all your guilt, who heals every one of your ills, who redeems your life from the grave, who crowns you with love and compassion. The Lord is compassion and love, slow to anger and rich in mercy. He does not treat us according to our sins nor repay us according to our faults. (*Responsorial Psalm 102*).

"My dear people, let us love one another since love comes from God...God's love for us was revealed when He sent into the world His only Son to be the sacrifice that takes our sins away...Since God has loved us so much, we too should love one another...As long as we love one another, God will live in us and his love will be complete in us." (*Second Reading, Jn 4:7-16*).

"I am the good shepherd. I know my own sheep and my own know me." (*Gospel Acclamation, Jn 10:14*).

Jesus spoke this parable to the scribes and pharisees: "What man among you with a hundred sheep, losing one, would not leave the ninety-nine in the wilderness and go after the missing one until he found it? And when he found it, would he not joyfully take it on his shoulders and then, when he got home, call together his friends and neighbours? 'Rejoice with me,' he would say. 'I have found my sheep that was lost.' In the same way I tell you, there will be more rejoicing in heaven over one repentant sinner than over ninety-nine virtuous men who have no need of repentance." (*Gospel, Lk 15:3-7*).

Reflection

The silly sheep which has wandered off is vulnerable to attack, frightened and helplessly longing for the call of its shepherd to safe, green pastures. When the shepherd finds it, it is so exhausted and forlorn that he carries its considerable bulk on his shoulders back to the sheepfold. Our Lord who is a Good Shepherd and not at all like those leaders who offend God by their infidelity (*cf. Ez 34*), deliberately startled His listeners. No shepherd in his right mind would endanger his entire flock, risk severe penalties for the sake of one stray, carry it home, and then want to throw a party. Friends and neighbours, especially weary fellow shepherds would not have appreciated being disturbed by such news. Divine foolishness, however, is greater than human wisdom, and the Sacred Heart's love is so inexhaustible that Jesus goes to unimaginable lengths to ensure that not one of His flock is lost. There is no suggestion that those who remain in the flock are less worthy, nor is there criticism of those who have already had a genuine change of heart. God does not make distinctions among His children, but there is intense joy in Heaven when an errant child returns to the Father.

In the light of the immensity of the universe and the innumerable generations of humanity, we may not consider ourselves to be of much significance, but God loves us infinitely more than we love ourselves.

DIVINE MERCY

Second Sunday of Easter, formerly "Low" Sunday.

Origins and significance

Sister Faustina (Helena Kowalska, 1905-1938) was a Polish Sister of Our Lady of Mercy in the convent of Plock and received visions of Our Lord for seven years. Her diary records the first occasion, February 22nd, 1931, when Our Lord appeared "clothed in a white garment, one hand raised in blessing, the other touching His white garment which was slightly open at the breast. From here emanated two large rays, one red, the other pale, symbolising blood and water." Our Lord told her to "paint an image, according to the pattern you see, with the signature 'Jesus, I trust you'. I desire this image to be venerated, first in your chapel and then throughout the world. I promise that the soul who will veneate this image will not perish...I desire that there should be a solemn Feast of Mercy on the first Sunday after Easter, when the image will be blessed and the priest will preach about God's unfathomable mercy." According to Sister Faustina's diary, which reveals her conviction that devotion to God's mercy will inspire a renewal of the spiritual life, Our Lord desired that the Feast should be preceded by a Novena based upon the Chaplet of Divine Mercy, and that the most suitable nine days would be the period from Good Friday to the Sunday after Easter.

The Novena Chaplet was to use the Rosary, the Our Father, Hail Mary and Apostles' Creed said on the introductory beads and then, on the large bead before each decade: "Eternal Father, I offer you the body, blood, soul and divinity of your dearly beloved Son, Our Lord Jesus Christ in atonement for our sins and the sins of the world." On each small bead of the decades is prayed; "For the sake of His sorrowful Passion, have mercy on us and on the world." After five decades, a final doxology is said three times: "Holy God, Holy Mighty One, Holy Immortal One, have mercy on us and on the world." To offer Our Lord to His Father is to unite ourselves with the sacrifice He offered for our salvation. In union with him, we acknowledge God's love for all people demonstrated by Our Lord in His Passion which calls for our forgiveness of one another and our own compassion for all His children. The words "For the sake of His sorrowful Passion" reflect the love Our lord showed for us in His death upon the Cross which is the strength of our prayer for Divine Mercy

Sister Faustina worked tirelessly to fulfil Our Lord's wishes before her holy death in 1938 and the devotion she fostered was brought to England in the early years of the Second World War. Pope John Paul II looks on Divine

Mercy as the image of his pontificate and its message as an antidote to the ills of the modern world. His appreciation recalls Pope John XXIII's initiation of a new openness to the world, "aggiornamento", using the "medicine of mercy" rather than condemnation. In his encyclical 'Rich in Mercy', 1980, the Pope wrote, "the more human conscience succumbs to secularisation, loses its sense of the the word 'mercy', moves away from God, and distances itself from the mystery of mercy, the more the Church has the right and duty to appeal to the God of mercy." He canonised Sister Faustina on April 30th, 2000, the first saint of the new millennium, and said her life was a gift of God for our time. A month later, he decreed that the Second Sunday of Easter would, henceforth, be celebrated as Divine Mercy Sunday.

Thanks to the international Divine Mercy movement, the devotion has blossomed throughout the Church, not least because Our Lord's choice of date for the Feast has theological significance in that Divine Mercy is reflected in His Passion and Death. The liturgical theme of the Easter Triduum and Easter Octave is His suffering, death and resurrection in the mystery of Redemption, and it appropriately culminates on the Second Sunday of Easter with the worship of God and His endless mercy.

From the Liturgy

"God of mercy, you wash away our sins in water, you give us new birth in the Spirit, and redeem us in the blood of Christ. As we celebrate Christ's Resurrection, increase our awareness of these blessings and renew your gift of life in us." (*Opening Prayer*).

The Gospel of the Feast (*Jn 20:19-31*) tells the story of Our Lord's gift of the Sacrament of Reconciliation, mercy and forgiveness. On the evening of the first Easter Sunday, the Apostles were daring to hope that Jesus had come back to life just as He had promised. Peter and John had inspected the empty tomb, Mary Magdalen had told them of her meeting with the Lord, and He had appeared to Peter. Then Clopas and, some say, Luke, had left Jerusalem for their homes in Emmaus six miles away in an attempt to cope with their grief and disappointment, and on the way they met a fellow traveller they did not at first recognise. He had walked with them as far as the village, had supper with them and, at last, revealed Himself in the breaking of bread. They rushed back with news too good to seem true to the Apostles who, apart from Thomas who was elsewhere, had taken refuge in the Cenacle. They were aware that rumours of the empty tomb and malicious reports that they had stolen Jesus' body were circulating in Jerusalem, and they feared for their lives.

Suddenly, Our Lord was with them, His glorified body needing no open door. He greeted them with His peace and showed the wounds of His hands and side to prove His identity. He told them that, as the Father had sent Him, the Incarnate Word, so now He was sending them to continue His mission. Like God breathing life into Adam at the Creation, He now breathed on them to communicate the Holy spirit in anticipation of the gifts of Pentecost, and entrusted them with the power to forgive sin on His behalf. On history's most glorious day, the Sacrament of Reconciliation was instituted as a sign of the peace He brings and the assurance of His Father's mercy.

"Eternal God, in whom mercy is endless and the treasury of compassion inexhaustible, look kindly upon us and increase your mercy in us so that, in difficult moments, we might not despair, nor become despondent, but with great confidence submit ourselves to your holy will which is love and mercy itself." (*Prayer of Sister Faustina*).

The Triumph of the Cross

September 14th

Origins and significance

This Feast marks the transformation of a cruel instrument of torture and humiliation into the sign of the victorious Redeemer who had saved and liberated humanity. Formerly the "Exaltation of the Cross", it has its origin in the discovery of the True Cross by St Helena, the mother of the emperor Constantine, during excavations preparatory to the building of a basilica on Calvary. This was confirmed by St Cyril of Jerusalem who died in 346, six years after St Helena, and the fourth century pilgrim, Egeria noted in her diary (*cf. Palm Sunday*) that the Feast was celebrated in Jerusalem to honour the discovery and involved the elevation of the Cross with blessing towards the four quarters of the compass.

The devotion came to Rome, where the basilica of Santa Croce was built to treasure the tree on which Our Lord forgave His executioners and sacrificed Himself for friends and enemies alike. It was soon adopted throughout the West where many churches were dedicated to "St Cross" or "Holy Cross". Place names like Holyrood Abbey in Scotland, Holy Cross in Hereford, and St Cross in Winchester will have a familiar ring. Anglo-Saxon devotion is exemplified in Caedmon's 'Dream of the Rood', the moving poem about his vision of the Cross and his reaction to what its voice says to him. Another poem 'Elene' (c.796) by Cynewulf, commemorates St Helena's discovery, and there are later stories of the Cross in 'The Golden Legend', an illustrated manual of mediaeval, ecclesiastical law, an edition of which was produced on William Caxton's printing-press.

The choice of September 14th for the Feast is related to the vision which Constantine received on the eve of the Battle of Milvian Bridge in 312. He saw a cross in the sky and beneath the words "*In hoc signo vinces*, In this sign you will be victorious", and success the following day prompted the selection of the date. Until the revision of the Calendar another feast on May 3rd remembered the Finding of the True Cross by St Helena.

From the Liturgy

"On the way through the wilderness, the Israelites lost patience. They spoke against God and Moses. 'Why did you bring us out of Egypt to die in this wilderness? There is neither bread nor water here; we are sick of this unsatisfying food.' At this, God sent fiery serpents among the people; their bite brought death to many in Israel. The people came and said to Moses, 'We have sinned by speaking against the Lord and against you. Intercede for us with the Lord to save us from these serpents.' Moses interceded for the people, and the Lord answered him, 'Make a fiery serpent and put it on a standard. If anyone is bitten and looks at it, he shall live. 'So Moses fashioned a bronze serpent and put it on a standard, and if anyone was bitten by a serpent, he looked at the bronze serpent and lived." (*First Reading, Nb21:4-9*)

"The state of Jesus was divine, yet he did not cling to His equality with God but emptied Himself to assume the condition of a slave, and became as men are; and being as all men are, He was humbler yet, even to accepting death, death on a cross." (*Second Reading, Ph 2:6-10*).

"Father, the suffering and death of your Son brought life to the whole world…The power of the Cross reveals your judgement on this world and the Kingship of Christ crucified. Though He was sinless, He suffered willingly for sinners. Though innocent, He accepted death to save the guilty. By His dying He destroyed our sins; by His rising, He has raised us up to holiness of life. You decreed that man should be saved through the wood of the Cross. The tree of man's defeat becomes His tree of victory; where life was lost, there life has been restored." (*From the Prefaces of the Passion and the Triumph of the Cross*).

Reflection

Not for the first time, the people were ungrateful for being freed from the slavery of Egypt and complained about the hardships of their journey back to the Promised Land. They were punished by attacks from serpents described as "fiery" because their bites caused inflammation, an echo here of Satan's disguise as the venomous serpent in Eden. When they acknowledged their sin, God took pity on them and told Moses to make a bronze serpent and raise it on a staff, so that anyone bitten could look at it and be healed. In the Gospel of the Feast (*Jn 3:13-17*), Our Lord himself tells us that this is a figure of His being elevated on the Cross to draw all things to Himself. He said to Nicodemus, "The Son of Man must be lifted up as Moses lifted up the serpent in the desert so that everyone who believes may have eternal life in Him." The necessity of Our Lord's redeeming death by being exalted on the Cross is proclaimed. The bronze serpent was a divine remedy for the bite of the poisonous serpent and preserved temporal life. The sinless Saviour, in the likeness of sinful flesh, heals the poisonous wounds of sin and gives everlasting life.

St Paul reflects that although Our Lord was one with God, He did not cling to an equality which was already His. The Divine Person chose to become one with fallen and vulnerable human nature, to the extent that He subjected Himself to the ultimate degradation of a slave's death by crucifixion. Satan used the wood of a tree and its fruit to deceive and enslave the human race; on the wood of the Cross the Second Adam redeemed the human race and restored it to friendship with God.

CHRIST THE KING

Thirty-fourth Sunday of the Year

Origins and significance

Pius XI, Pope from 1922-39, instituted the Feast in 1925 to counter secularism, atheism, communism, and the extremes of nationalism. It remembers that Our Lord, given all power "in Heaven and on earth", has supreme authority and kingship over earthly politics and governments. It celebrates the anointed King who conquered suffering and death to bring humanity from darkness to His universal Kingdom of Light. He is the epitome of all the best qualities of the shepherd-kings of old, whose royalty lay in service to their people and leading them to the Kingdom of God and His Justice.

The Feast looks to the ultimate, blessed destination to which God calls all creation and, appropriately, it brings the Church's liturgical year to a triumphant conclusion. Our Lord is hailed as Messiah-King, to whom all persons and institutions are subordinate and who, by redeeming us, has opened to us the gates of His Kingdom. Closely associated with His royal dignity is His appointment by God to judge the living and the dead, for He is the perfection of justice, integrity and mercy who knows the human hearts He has created.

From the Liturgy

"The Lord (who had become saddened by the self-seeking infidelity of Israel's leaders) says, 'I am going to look after my flock myself...rescue them from wherever they have been scattered during the mist and darkness...I shall pasture my sheep and show them where to rest...look for the lost one...bandage the wounded and make the weak strong. I shall watch over the fat and healthy. I shall be a true shepherd to them...I will judge between sheep and sheep, between rams and goats.'"

"I saw coming on the clouds of heaven, one like a son of man. He came to the one of great age and was led into his presence. On him was conferred sovereignty, glory and kingship, and men of all peoples...became his servants. His sovereignty is an eternal sovereignty which will never pass away, nor will his empire be destroyed."

"The Lord said to David, 'You are the man who shall be shepherd of my people Israel, you shall be the leader of Israel.' So all the elders...in the presence of the Lord...anointed David king of Israel." (*First Readings, Ez 34:12, 15-17; Dn 7:13-14; 2S 5:1-3*).

"Just as all men die in Adam, so all men will be brought to life in Christ; but all of them in their proper order: Christ as the first-fruits and then, after the coming of Christ, those who belong to Him. After that will come the end, when He hands over the kingdom to God the Father, having done away with every sovereignty, authority and power. For he must be king until He has put all His enemies under His feet and the last of the enemies to be destroyed is death. And when everything is subjected to Him, then the Son Himself will be subject in His turn to the One who subjects all things to Him, so that God may be all in all."

"Jesus Christ is the First-born from the dead, the Ruler of the kings of the earth...to Him be glory and power for ever...It is He who is coming on the clouds; everyone will see Him... 'I am the Alpha and the Omega' says the Lord God who is, who was, and who is to come." (*Second Readings, 1 Cor 15:20-26,28; Rv 1:5-8*)

"Father, you anointed your only Son, Jesus Christ with the oils of gladness, as the eternal priest and universal king. As priest He offered His life on the altar of the cross and redeemed the human race by this one, perfect sacrifice of peace. As King He claims dominion over all creation, that He may present to you an eternal and universal kingdom of truth, holiness, and grace, justice, love, and peace." (*Preface of the Feast*).

Reflection
(cf. Mt 25; 31-46; Jn 18:33-37; Lk 23:35-43).

The reading from Matthew's Gospel is about the end of Our Lord's ministry and His very last parable before His crucifixion and death. The solemn opening describes how the Son of Man will come in glory to separate the good from the bad, the sheep from the goats. The criterion for admission to His Kingdom is simple: "I was hungry and you gave me food" and "as you did this to one of the least of these brothers of mine, you did it to me." Neither sheep nor goats knew that it was Our Lord to whom they were, or were not, responding when a fellow human was in need, so the analogy highlights a connection between how we use our daily lives, and the conclusion we reach about our performance when all is revealed on the day of Judgement. It also emphasises Christ the King's concern with justice, love and peace for the well-being of all men and women, especially those who are hungry, thirsty, naked, alienated, or imprisoned. Here there is His preferential option for the poor, and His exhortation that those who belong to the Kingdom should share His tenderness for those in need. Significantly, Matthew points out that this was the last thing Our Lord wanted to say. (*cf. Mt 26:1*).

Christ the King came to serve and give His life as a ransom for many. He washed His disciples feet because He came among them as one who serves and not as the one who sits at the table waiting to be served. Rather than pursue earthly influence, He reaches out and gives Himself to the poor, sick, despised, ostracised, and sinners so that they are comforted, healed, pardoned, and brought to salvation. His loving service, characterised by humility and obedience, culminates in His passion. When Pilate asked him if He were the King of the Jews, He did not reject the title but explained that His Kingdom was of another world. When they had scourged Him cruelly, the soldiers mocked Him as "King of the Jews" and told Him that, if He were, then He should save Himself. It was a thief, a fellow crucifixion sufferer, who, despite all indications to the contrary, recognised His true nature. He asked to be remembered when Our Lord took possession of His Kingdom, and his faith was rewarded with the promise of Paradise. The Saviour, obedient unto a shameful death on the Cross, is now exalted to enthroned glory at God's right hand, and given a name which is above all other names. (*cf. Mt 27:37; Mk 10:45; Lk 22:27, 23:37, 42-43; Jn 18:33, 36*).

ACKNOWLEDGMENTS

The CTS gratefully acknowledges use of prayers, scripture quotations and hymns from;

The Jerusalem Bible (Darton, Longman and Todd, London, 1974), *Catechism of the Catholic Church* (Geoffrey Chapman, London, 1994), *The Divine Office* (Collins, London, 1974), *The Psalms, A New Translation* (The Grail (England) published by Collins, 1963), *Papal Documents* (Catholic Truth Society, London), *Westminster Hymnal* (Burns, Oates and Washbourne, London, 1948), and *Catholic Commentary on the Holy Scripture* (Thomas Nelson and Sons, London. 1951).

Chronological List of Feasts

The Nativity of the Lord December 25th

The Holy Family of Jesus, Mary and Joseph Sunday in the Octave of Christmas, or December 30th if no Sunday intervenes.

The Circumcision of the Lord Once a Holy Day of Obligation on January 1st

The Most Holy Name of Jesus Formerly the Sunday between the Circumcision and the Epiphany

The Epiphany of the Lord January 6th

The Baptism of the Lord Sunday after the Epiphany

The Presentation of the Lord February 2nd

The Annunciation of the Lord March 25th

The Resurrection Easter Sunday

Divine Mercy Second Sunday of Easter, formerly "Low" Sunday.

The Ascension Thursday of the Sixth Week of Easter

The Body and Blood of Christ Thursday after Trinity Sunday

The Sacred Heart of Jesus Friday after the Second Sunday after Pentecost

The Transfiguration of the Lord August 6th

The Triumph of the Cross September 14th

Christ the King Thirty-fourth Sunday of the Year